BARBIE DEVELOPER

Ruth Handler

LEE SLATER

Checkerboard Library

An Imprint of Abdo Publishing
abdopublishing.com

abdopublishing.com

Printed in the United States of America, North Mankato, Minnesota
102015
012016

THIS BOOK CONTAINS
RECYCLED MATERIALS

Content Developer: Nancy Tuminelly
Design and Production: Mighty Media, Inc.
Series Editor: Paige Polinsky
Cover Photos: AP Images/Corbis (center); Mighty Media (border)
Interior Photos: Alamy, p. 26; AP Images, pp. 4, 9, 18–19, 25, 28 (bottom left); AP Images/Corbis, p. 13; Bianca Anne Martins, p. 14; Corbis, pp. 12, 15, 16, 17, 28 (bottom right), 29 (bottom left); Courtesy of the Beck Archives, Special Collections, University Libraries, University of Denver, p. 5; iStockphoto, pp. 21, 22, 27, 29; Kelli Barron/Logopedia, p. 28 (top right); Shutterstock, pp. 6, 23, 29 (bottom right); Superstock, p. 10

Library of Congress Cataloging-in-Publication Data
Names: Slater, Lee, 1969- author.
Title: Barbie developer : Ruth Handler / by Lee Slater.
Description: Minneapolis, MN : Abdo Publishing, 2016. | Series: Toy
   trailblazers | Includes index.
Identifiers: LCCN 2015028646 | ISBN 9781624039744
Subjects: LCSH: Handler, Ruth--Juvenile literature. | Doll makers--United
   States--Biography--Juvenile literature. | Barbie dolls--Juvenile literature.
   | Mattel, Inc.--Juvenile literature.
Classification: LCC NK4894.2.H324 S57 2016 | DDC 338.4/76887221092--dc23
LC record available at http://lccn.loc.gov/2015028646

CONTENTS

Chapter 1

GROWING Up

On November 4, 1916, in Denver, Colorado, Ruth Marianna Mosko was born. She was the youngest in a family of ten children. This baby grew up to be Ruth Handler. She would invent the Barbie doll, the most famous and popular doll in the world!

Ruth's parents were Jewish **immigrants**. Her father, Jacob, came to the United States from Poland in 1907. His wife, Ida, arrived with their children in 1909. They were eager to come to a new country where there was no war. When they reached Denver, they knew they had found a place to call home. Like so

Ruth Handler learned many important business skills as a child that would help her develop and sell her world-famous invention, the Barbie doll.

Ruth

many other **immigrants**, they hoped to live the **American dream**.

Reaching for the American dream required a lot of hard work. Jacob and Ida were very busy working and raising Ruth's siblings. They sent Ruth to live with their eldest child, Sarah.

Sarah's husband, Louie, owned a drugstore. When Ruth was ten years old, she began working in the store. The job introduced Ruth to the idea of **merchandising**. The skills she learned in the drugstore would later help her sell millions of Barbie dolls!

5

Chapter 2

Into the WORLD

During the 1930s, people loved going to the movies. Hollywood, California, was famous for being the movie-making capital of the United States. Actors and actresses were major celebrities, and many girls dreamed of becoming movie stars.

Ruth loved all the glamour and style of Hollywood.

When she was 19 years old, Ruth moved to Hollywood. She worked as a **stenographer** at Paramount, one of Hollywood's most famous movie studios. She even saw movie stars every now and then! Hollywood was a very exciting place to live in the 1930s.

Ruth's high school boyfriend, Elliot Handler, came to visit her in Hollywood. He ended up staying in California for a year. Ruth and Elliot then returned to Denver. Ruth worked as a secretary for her brother Joe. After Ruth and Elliot married in 1938, they moved back to California.

Elliot studied **industrial** design at The Art Center College of Design in Pasadena, California. Handler went back to work at Paramount. Before their daughter, Barbara, was born in 1941, Handler left her job at the movie studio. She and Elliot started a business making products such as jewelry and candleholders out of plastic. By the time their son, Kenneth, was born in 1944, the Handlers had a successful business.

Chapter 3

Mattel Creations
IS BORN

In 1944, the Handlers were ready to make a change. They sold the plastics business and came up with a new idea. At first they made picture frames. Elliot was in charge of design and production. Handler was responsible for **marketing**. She advertised and sold the products that Elliot manufactured.

Elliot's friend Harold "Matt" Matson liked to design and build things too. In 1945, the Handlers and Matson started a company. They called it Mattel Creations. The name Mattel was a combination of the names Matt and Elliot.

Handler and Matson made dollhouse furniture. But they had the most fun making toys. So they decided that Mattel Creations would make and sell toys. Mattel's Uke-a-Doodle, a miniature **ukulele**, quickly became a success. Their toys were a hit!

Matson left the company after a few years, and the Handlers became the sole partners. They hired employees, opened offices, and contracted

Ruth and Elliot Handler at their Mattel office in front of a case of toys they produced

with factories to manufacture the toys. By 1955, Mattel Company was advertising its toys on television. *The Mickey Mouse Club* was the most popular children's show at the time. Mattel was the program's **exclusive sponsor**. Now kids all over the United States knew about and wanted Mattel toys. Business was great!

FUN FACT

The inventor of the world's most famous doll later said she never played with dolls at all!

Chapter 4

BYE-BYE
Baby Dolls

In the 1950s, teenage fashion dolls looked very similar to toddler dolls. Handler's daughter, Barbara, and her friends were bored with these dolls. They played with paper dolls instead. Paper dolls were figures cut out of paper with clothes that

By the 1950s, paper dolls came in many different styles. But Handler knew she could invent a doll that was more fun for older girls to play with.

FUN FACT

Barbie's real name is Barbara Millicent Roberts. She was named after Handler and Elliot's daughter, Barbara.

were cut from paper too. The clothes were attached to the dolls with folding tabs.

The girls loved making up stories for their paper dolls. While watching them, Handler understood that they were imagining their own futures. Handler believed that this was a **crucial** part of growing up. "My whole philosophy of Barbie was that through the doll, the little girl could be anything she wanted to be," wrote Handler in her autobiography, *Dream Doll: The Ruth Handler Story*.

Handler wished the girls could have grown-up dolls that weren't made out of paper. She wanted them to have plastic dolls that could wear the latest fashions. Maybe Mattel Creations could make a doll like this.

Chapter 5

Barbie's RELATIVE

In 1952, cartoonist Reinhard Beuthien created a character for a newspaper in Hamburg, Germany. Her name was Lilli. She was classy, **fashionable**, and attractive. Because Lilli was so popular, Beuthien decided to produce a Lilli doll.

In 1956, the Handlers took a trip to Europe with their teenage children. When Ruth saw the Lilli doll in a shop, she was very excited. This was exactly the kind of doll she wanted to make!

Handler bought one Lilli doll for Barbara and two for the designers at Mattel. She wanted them to make a doll that was very similar. Many

Lilli dolls were hand painted and very fragile.

staff members at Mattel were not very excited. They didn't think anyone would want to buy a doll that looked like a grown-up. But Handler insisted that it would sell. So Mattel Creations got to work creating the doll that would become Barbie.

13

Chapter 6

SUCCESS!

Barbie Teenage Fashion Model made her first appearance at the American International Toy Fair on March 9, 1959. It was held in New York City. At first, the toy buyers were **skeptical**. They had never seen a doll that wasn't a baby or toddler. Would girls really want to play with a doll that had adult features?

Handler believed in her idea. She knew girls would love Barbie. Handler made a TV commercial, and the Barbie doll was an instant success. Young girls begged their local toy stores to carry Barbie dolls. The dolls sold out as soon as they reached the shelves.

FUN FACT

Barbie is from the fictional town of Willows, Wisconsin.

At first, the factories struggled to meet the **demand** for the new toy. More than 350,000 Barbie dolls were sold within one year. Barbie was already the best-selling doll of all time. Handler had given girls a whole new way to play, and they loved it!

When Barbie was created in the late 1950s, girls admired the famous movie stars of the time. Elizabeth Taylor and Marilyn Monroe were talented, glamorous, and popular. The first Barbie was designed to look like a movie star. But she would go on to be many other things!

The first Barbie doll wore a black-and-white striped, one-piece swimsuit, sunglasses, and sandals. She was available with long blonde or brunette hair styled in a ponytail.

Chapter 7

Barbie Reflects CULTURE

Handler was a **marketing** expert. She knew consumers would want the latest Barbie fashions. **Updating** Barbie's clothes would increase the company's sales.

In the early 1960s, Barbie wore classic **outfits** inspired by Jackie Kennedy. The wife of President John F. Kennedy was a style icon. Barbie later joined the Mod Era. This was a time when many young people wore colorful, casual clothing, tinted sunglasses, and blue jeans.

Many of the popular TV shows of the 1970s took place in California. The fun, relaxed beach **lifestyle** was appealing to many people. In 1971, Malibu Barbie was born, with her suntan, cool beach clothes, and streaked blonde hair.

Handler knew that Barbie needed clothes, hairstyles, and accessories that changed with the times.

In the 1980s, when MTV first came on the scene, Barbie became a rock star. Her band was Barbie and the Rockers. Together they rocked the leggings, neon colors, and bold makeup of the era.

The big trends of the 1990s were shoulder pads and huge hair. Totally Hair Barbie took this to another level, featuring nearly 11-inch (28 cm) **tresses**! And in the 2000s, she favored denim, **pastel** colors, and stick-on fashion jewels.

Chapter 8

WORK & PLAY

Some people thought Barbie dolls showed girls a limited choice of future careers. This was not at all what Handler had in mind when she created Barbie. She wanted a fun and positive role model for girls. Over time, Barbie proved that she was more than a fashion doll.

Barbie had a variety of jobs in the 1970s. She was an actress, surgeon, and United Airlines flight attendant. She also had careers in the sports industry. These included Olympic athlete, downhill skier, and figure skater.

During the 1980s, more women were entering professional careers. In the past, many of these jobs had typically been performed by men. Some of Barbie's careers at this time included business executive, doctor, and army officer.

By 1992, nearly every job and profession was open to women. Barbie's

FUN FACT

A Barbie doll is in the official "America's Time Capsule" that was buried in 1976 at the celebration of the US Bicentennial.

careers in the 1990s included engineer, police officer, firefighter, and NASCAR driver. Today, Barbie can choose from over 120 careers! She has been an architect, news anchor, **paleontologist**, and much more.

When Barbie became an astronaut in 1965, she showed girls that the sky's the limit!

Chapter 9

Life of a BARBIE DOLL

By 1967, Ruth Handler was president of Mattel. Besides Barbie, Ken, and her friends and family, Mattel sold many other toys. The Chatty Cathy doll and Hot Wheels cars were very popular products. Mattel was the world's leading toy manufacturer.

Today, it takes a team of more than 100 people to design a new look for Barbie! And the designers are always looking for fresh ideas. They collect pictures from magazines that show clothing styles, fabrics, makeup, hairstyles, and **accessories**. All the ideas are posted on what they call the "**inspiration** board."

Mattel's offices in Hong Kong, China, determine the doll's price. A factory then manufactures the dolls. They are shipped all over the world. This entire process, from the idea to the store, takes anywhere from 3 to 18 months.

Barbie's Style

HAIR

Hair experts color, cut, and style Barbie's hair to match the design.

MAKEUP

Makeup artists paint Barbie's lips, eyes, and cheeks the perfect colors.

OUTFIT

Fashion illustrators and pattern makers work together to design the perfect **outfit**.

ACCESSORIES

Shoes, purses, and other **accessories** complete the new look.

Chapter 10

The Barbie
BUSINESS

The original Barbie Teenage Fashion Model was **revolutionary.** But without new **updates** and features, girls would have soon become bored with the doll. And Mattel would not be the success that it is today.

Mattel's world headquarters in El Segundo, California

When Handler invented Barbie's friends, she was doing more than giving Barbie companions. She was also creating a business opportunity for Mattel. With more characters, the company could make and sell more toys.

Fun **accessories** also increase sales. The Barbie Dream House is one example of a Barbie accessory that sold very well. The pink convertible car is another popular accessory.

Throughout the years, Barbie never ages. However, in keeping with Handler's original vision, Barbie does change with the times. She loves exploring different jobs and fashion trends. It's fun to give Barbie a new **outfit** and a new role to play.

Thanks to Handler's **marketing** genius, there is always a new Barbie doll to buy. There are also always new outfits, accessories, and DVDs. These are fun for the girls who love Barbie, and good business for Mattel!

Chapter 11

REAL LIFE

Barbie's world is much simpler than real life. In 1970, Handler was diagnosed with breast **cancer**. She needed to have surgery to remove her breasts. The surgery cured Handler, but she had to adjust to her new appearance. She wished for a product that would help her feel confident again.

Ruth and Elliot left Mattel in 1975. Barbie was an international success, and the best-selling toy in world history. The Handlers had earned a lot of money since they sold their first Barbie doll. Now it was time for a new project.

In 1976, Handler invented the product she had wished for a few years earlier. She started a business called Nearly Me. Her invention was a **silicone** breast **prosthesis** that looked natural and felt comfortable. Her invention helped many female cancer survivors have more confidence in their appearance. In 1991, she sold this company to Spenco Medical Corporation.

On April 27, 2002, Handler died at the age of 85. Her husband lived for another nine years. He died on July 21, 2011, at the age of 95.

In 1994, Handler (*left*) helped celebrate Barbie's thirty-fifth birthday. There, she took a photo with Kristi Cooke (*right*), an actress dressed as Barbie.

Chapter 12

Handler's LEGACY

Handler lived the **American dream** just as her parents had hoped. As the inventor of the most recognized doll in the world, she became famous and wealthy. The key to her success was a combination of imagination and hard work.

More than 1 billion Barbie dolls have been sold since 1959. Girls all over the world own Barbie dolls, and many grown women have them, too. Handler once said, "She is more than a doll to them, whatever their age. She has become a part of them."

Barbie fulfilled Ruth Handler's dream of letting girls play while using their imaginations. Barbie could be

In 2002, Barbara Handler added Barbie's footprints and handprints to California's famous Hollywood Walk of Fame.

anything she wanted to be.
The children who played with
Barbie gained confidence.
They could have big dreams
for their own futures too.

As Barbie keeps
evolving, she will always
be an important part of
popular **culture**. What's
next for Barbie? Who
knows! But she'll always
be on the leading edge of
fashion trends and career
opportunities!

Barbie has helped girls imagine
themselves as coaches, architects,
doctors, pilots, teachers, and even
presidential candidates!

TIMELINE

1916
Ruth Marianna Mosko is born in Denver, Colorado, on November 4.

1941
Daughter Barbara Handler is born.

1945
Mattel Creations is founded by Elliot Handler, Harold Matson, and Ruth Handler.

1938
Ruth Mosko and Elliot Handler are married.

1944
Son Kenneth Handler is born.

1956
Handler finds the doll that inspires Barbie while vacationing in Europe.

Ken and Barbie broke up on Valentine's Day, 2004.
They got back together seven years later, on Valentine's Day, 2011.

1959

Handler invents the Barbie doll and introduces her at the American International Toy Fair in New York City.

1970

Handler is diagnosed with breast cancer.

1976

Handler starts a new business called Nearly Me.

1967

Handler becomes president of Mattel.

1975

The Handlers leave Mattel Company.

2002

Ruth Handler dies on April 27.

Glossary

accessory – a small item that you wear with your clothes, such as a belt, gloves, or scarf.

American dream – a life of happiness and prosperity desired by many American citizens.

cancer – any of a group of often deadly diseases marked by harmful changes in the normal growth of cells. Cancer can spread and destroy healthy tissues and organs.

crucial – extremely important for the success of something.

culture – the customs, arts, and tools of a nation or a people at a certain time.

demand – the amount of an available product that buyers are willing and able to purchase.

evolve – to develop gradually.

exclusive sponsor – a person or company that pays the costs of a radio or television broadcast in return for having their products advertised.

fashionable – liked and admired by many people at a particular time.

immigrant – a person who enters another country to live.

industrial – of or having to do with factories and making things in large quantities.

inspiration – something that fills someone with an emotion, an idea, or an attitude.

lifestyle – the way a being, group, or society lives.

marketing – the process of advertising or promoting something so people will want to buy it.

merchandising – the act of trying to sell goods by advertising them or displaying them attractively.

outfit – pieces of clothing that are worn together.

paleontologist – a scientist who deals with fossils and other ancient life forms, especially dinosaurs.

pastel – a light, soft shade of a color.

prosthesis – an artificial device that replaces a missing part of a body.

revolution – a sudden, radical, or far-reaching change.

silicone – a stable chemical compound containing silicon, used for making plastics, lubricants, and artificial body parts.

skeptical – having an attitude of doubt or disbelief.

stenographer – a person whose job is to write down someone's spoken words by using a special type of writing.

tresses – a woman's or girl's hair, especially when it is worn long and loose.

ukulele – a small, four-stringed guitar originally made popular in Hawaii.

update – to make something more modern or up to date.

Index